Alchemical Hieroglyphics

WHICH WERE CAUSED TO BE PAINTED
UPON AN ARCH IN ST. INNOCENTS CHURCH YARD
IN PARIS BY:

Nicholas Flammel

Translated out of the French in 1624 by:
EIRENAEUS ORANDUS

HEPTANGLE GILLETTE BOOKS
MCMLXXX

LIBRARY OF CONGRESS CATALOGUE CARD NUMBER: 80-82537
ISBN: 0-935214-04-6

PRINTED & BOUND BY: HEPTANGLE BOOKS
P. O. BOX 283 BERKELEY HEIGHTS, NJ 07922

Table of Contents

List of Illustrations — vii
Translator's Dedication — ix
Preface by W. W. Westcott — xiii

Flammel's Alchemical Hieroglyphics

Invocation — 3
Introduction by Nicholas Flammel — 5
§1 Theological Interpetations of the Hieroglyphics — 27
§2 Philosophical Interpetations: the Furnace — 35
§3 Of the Sulphur & Mercury, the Male & Female — 43
§4 Of the union of the Sulphur & Mercury — 53
§5 On the symbolism of Decapitation, & of the Dissolution & Coagulation — 61
§6 On the Tripartite nature of the Stone — 71
§7 Of the Rubification — 77
§8 On the power of Multiplication — 81
§9 Of the full perfection of the Stone — 87

List of Illustrations

¶ Flammel's Fresco [fold-out plate]	x
¶ Alchemists at Work	xii
¶ Book Plate by Flammel	2

The Figures of Abraham the Jew

¶ A Caduceus formed of two snakes swallowing each other twined round a rod	7
¶ A Crucified Snake	8
¶ A Desert floor with springs & small snakes moving about	9
¶ Mercury holding a Caduceus; Saturn in a cloud armed with a Sythe	11
¶ On a mountain summit, a flower shaken by wind; about it Dragons & Griffins	12
¶ A Garden enclosed by hedges; in the midst an oak-stock & a golden leaved rose tree	13
¶ A King [Herod] orders the slaying of the Innocents; soldiers fill a vat with their blood and the Sun & the Moon bathe therin	14

The Figures of Nicholas Flammel

¶ The Philosophical Furnace	38
¶ Two Dragons, male & female	43
¶ A Man & a Woman with a rowl	53
¶ St. Paul holding a naked Sword; at his feet, a kneeling man with a rowl	62
¶ Christ coming to judge the World; beneath Him, three resuscitants arising from their graves	70
¶ Two Angels & their rowls	77
¶ St. Peter holding a Key; kneeling at his feet, a woman holding a rowl	82
¶ A Man holding the paws of a winged Lion	87

THE TRANSLATOR DEDICATES THIS WORK TO
THE MOST EXCELLENTLY ACCOMPLISHED
LADY, THE C. D. OE E.

READER

Part of these things thy mind shall prompt thee to,
And part, some God shall teach thee how to do.

AGAIN?

If Fate thee call, else with no violence,
Nor hardest Iron canst thou dig them thence,

OR AGAIN, & SO FAREWELL.

Many shapes of Fate there be,
Much done beyond our hope, we see:
What we think sure, God often stays
And finds, for things undreamt of, ways,
For so did this succeed to me,
And so I wish it may to thee.

EIRENAEUS ORANDUS

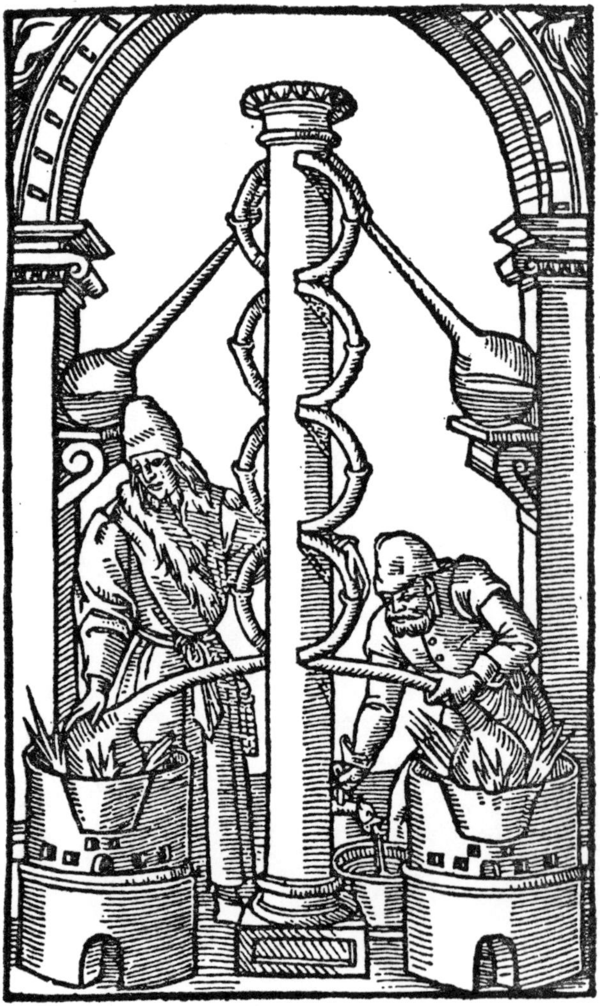

PREFACE

NO apology is needed for the study of the life, work and success of Nicholas Flamel. He was alike conspicuous by his riches, and by the excellent uses he made of them. The vast sums of money which he expended in charitable and public works have made his name famous and respected, even down to our own time. Many authors have written on the subject of his life attainments, but no one of them produces any record of a dishonest or wicked action. The only evil suggestion found among many volumes is, that as the nameless author cannot bring himself to believe in *"Transmutation"* he falls back on the imputation that Flamel made an enormous fortune by cheating the Jews; but of this there is not a scrap of evidence: and *some* persons might smile and say this process were harder than the former.

Especial interest attaches to the personality of Flamel for another reason—his wife Pernelle or Perrenella, became by his teaching and her own intuitions as learned and successful a mystic and occult operator as himself. As a fitting prelude to his description of the *Book of Abraham* and his own hieroglyphics, a few remarks on his history will be of interest.

Nicholas Flamel (or Flammel) was born in the year 1330, probably at Pontoise, in France: he received a good education and entered upon the important professon of a Scrivener and law-writer in Paris; the old French title was "escripvain," a word implying a writer and instructor in the more difficult and ornate caliography in use at that date; it would include the art of illuminating MSS, as well as the ordinary forms of every-day work, and a writer would also be the notary and the accountant of that day. The profession was an honourable one, but not a specially lucrative employment; although King John II of France was a literary King, and left three heirs who were alike book-learned bibliophiles, and who it is believed gave Flamel important work to carry out; of these Charles V, the Wise, succeeded to the throne in 1364.

Nicholas had a younger brother, Jean, who was also a writer, but with him we are not concerned. Nicholas Flamel married in 1356 (but some say 1370) a widow lady named Pernelle, she had some private property and was a charitable woman according to her means. They lived near the Church of St. Jacques la Boucherie, at the corner of the Rue des Ecrivains; and later in 1407 he built a house for himself and wife in the Rue de Montmorency; this building had a gable front, and he designed and executed a large hieroglyphical bas-relief across it.

They also built a splendid Arcade at the Cemetery of the Innocents in 1389, and in 1407 a second Arcade, or Portal to the Church of St. Jacques; on each of these buildings he placed curious designs of a mixed theological and alchemic meaning. Besides these more ornate works he and his wife built fourteen hostels for the poor, three chapels, and repaired seven Churches.

Pernelle died in 1397 and Flamel himself *appears* to have died in 1418; for his will is still extant, and by it he left the property of his wife and himself in trust to the Church of St. Jacques for the use of the poor.

By reason of his profession he was thrown at an early age among the libraries, and among authors and readers, and so he became a learned man at a period when erudition was a rarity. A vast number of Ancient and Mediæval MSS, were concerned with the ancient religious mythologies and with the secret or occult sciences, especially with Alchemy. Amid such surroundings he had, in 1357, unexpectedly offered to him for a trifle of 2 Florins a curious old Book, which he at once purchased. This slight event fixed his whole course of life. He studied it, by the light of all his learning, and his wife by her intuition, but they failed to grasp its meaning. The Volume had various diagrams; —he painted them on the walls of his house, and showed them to every one with any pretence to erudition: every-one failed to discern the mystery. He copied them on paper and started on a long pilgrimage hunting for an adept; at last, in Spain, he met one who knew their meaning and who returned with Flamel to see the work itself. Unfortunately, this occultist died before Paris was reached, but Flamel knew the *"Principle"* and the foundation was laid. Three years more study enabled himself and his wife, who was then of equal learning with himself, to gain the secret of the *"Preparation,"* and success was assured. On January 17th 1382, they made a first projection and a half-pound of Mercury became Pure Silver; again, on April 25th, they converted Mercury into Pure Gold.

In the fac-simile Reprint which follows this Preface, Flamel describes the *Book of Abraham* and its mystic contents; and then he describes and illustrates the meanings, both theological and Alchemical, of the Designs and Hieroglyphics which he himself erected on the public edifices I have before mentioned; which designs are alike capable of *Revealing* and *Reveiling* the Secrets of Transmutation.

The Frontispiece with its seven designs shows the 3 pictures of the 7th, 14, and 21st pages, with the 4 pictures on the 4th and 5th pages of the *Book of Abraham;* and they are more instructive than the pictures of Flamel himself interspersed among the letterpress; which, without this description are nearly valueless, their Religious meaning being so much more obvious than any other. Their special peculiarity consists of the colours allotted to the several parts, which it is not possible to reproduce.

Of Flamel's Work, chapter I may be set aside as simply religious; the remaining chapters refer to the "Mastery of Hermes" and are no doubt a real Alchemic Treatise. Flamel tells that unless we know the First Principle or Agent, his book is useless, because it only concerns the processes to be applied when the *Prima Materia* is known. Nevertheless it is an interesting study.

The 2nd chapter describes the furnace for the purpose of applying heat to the Philosophical Egg: then, especial precautions are given against extreme heat and also against too little Warmth; either extreme spoiling the powers.

In chapter 3 are described the two Dragons, the male and female sperms, the sulphur and mercury which under due conditions give birth to a Son, the Quintessence: putrefaction or Blackening must occur first, with a foul smell, or no result can be looked for. The full black should require 40 days, and any previous orange colour shows something is wrong.

Chapter 4 concerns the union of the two sexes, or seed, equivalent to the pure elements in combination; from the Blackness, as above, an earth now is produced; this will subsequently be Whiteness.

There is to be a division into two portions, *Azoth* and *Leton*; the former to wash the latter; then the white becomes achieved,—the most difficult process.

Chapter 5 explains the symbolism of decapitation, and the virtues of repeated dissolving and coagulating; five times a month to each process.

In chapter 6, the material changes colour to green, and a dissertation on the tripartite nature of the *Stone* is given.

Chapter 7 tells us the Red must be obtained, the Rubification by feeding the product with Virgin's milk of the Sun; iridescence is produced; the many hues of the peacock's tail precede the true Redness, and dry heat should not be checked until this appears.

Chapter 8;—under the Type of a woman the product seeks the power of Multiplication; then the Quintessence is obtained and our only risk is the loss of it by careless excess of heat.

Chapter 9 revels in the full perfection of the Stone, red and like a flying lion, beyond the power of heaven and all the powers represented in the Zodiac to destroy it.

According to *Penes nos unda Tagi,* an anagram of the famous Dr. Espagnet, the Great Work of the Philosophers should be commenced in the time of the Sun in Capricorn the former house of Saturn; the Black stage, or Head of the Crow comes on in about 40 days in Aquarius, the other house of Saturn: Sol coming into Pisces, the Blackness deepens: Sol entering Aries, the separation occurs: Cancer brings on the Whiteness because Luna reigns in White majesty in her house. In Leo, the work of Sol begins; and the glory of Redness is attained in Libra; Scorpio follows, and Saggitarius completes the Work in Jupiter's own dominion. I believe, however, this system is due to the skill of Raymond Lully. Serious enquirers should not fail to study the several works of Hermes Trismegistus, *Aureus,* from Dr. South's suppressed work; *Virgin of the World, Asclepios* and the *Divine Pymander,* which are in truth concerned in the same mystery; and the *Count de Gabalis,* which has a Sub-Title the "Extravagant mysteries of the Cabalists," is worth perusal, although the extravagance is not found in the matter suggested by the title, but in the manner of its presentation by the Abbe de Villars to the public.

W. W. WESTCOTT,
FRA. ROS. CRU. IX°.

LONDON,
NOVEMBER 1889.

THE EXPLICATION OF THE
HIEROGLYPHIC FIGURES.
Placed by me, NICHOLAS FLAMMEL, Scrivener,
in the Church-yard of the Innocents,
in the fourth Arch, entering by
the great gate of St. Dennis
Street, and taking the way
on the right hand.

LA BIBLE
DE MONSEIGNEUR
LE DUC DE BERRY

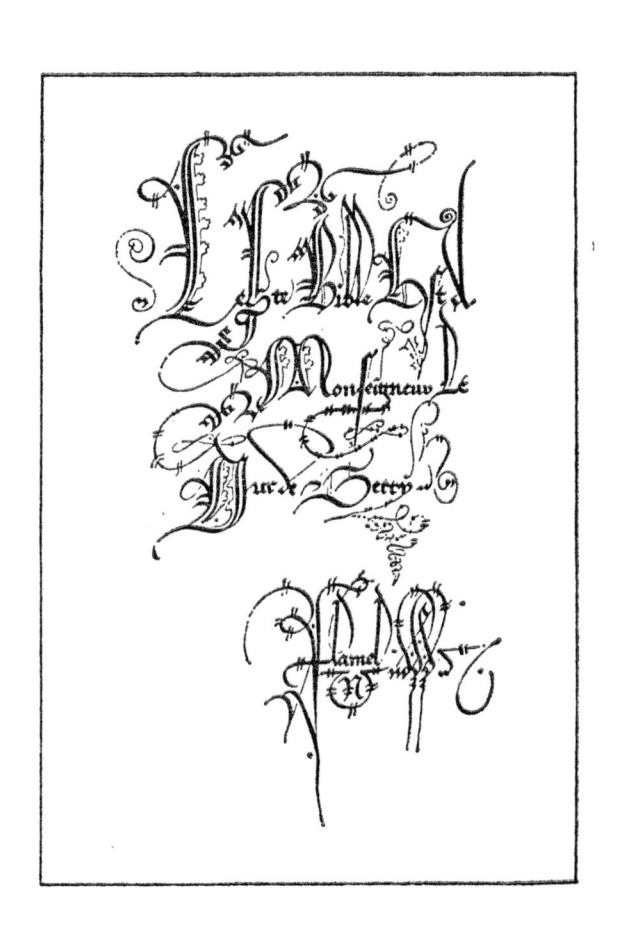

THE BOOK OF THE HIEROGLYPHICAL FIGURES OF NICHOLAS FLAMMEL.

ETERNALLY praised be the Lord my God, which lifteth the humble from the base dust, and maketh the hearts of such as hope in him to rejoice: which of his grace openeth to them that believe, the Springs of his bounty, and putteth under their feet the worldly Spheres (or circles) of all earthly happinesses: In him be always our trust; in his fear our felicity; in his mercy, the glory of the reparation of our nature, and in our prayers, our unshaken assurance. And thou, O God Almighty, as thy benignity hath vouchsafed to open upon earth before me (thy unworthy servant) all the treasures of the riches of the world; so may it please thy great clemency, then when I shall be no more in the number of the living, to open unto me the treasures of heaven, and to let me behold thy Divine face, the Majesty whereof is a delight unspeakable, and the ravishing joy whereof never ascended into the heart of living man. I ask it of thee, for our Lord Jesus Christ thy well beloved Son, his sake, who, in the unity of the Holy Spirit, liveth with thee world without end. Amen.

THE EXPLICATION OF THE
HIEROGLYPHIC FIGURES.
Placed by me, NICHOLAS FLAMMEL, Scrivener,
in the Church-yard of the Innocents,
in the fourth Arch, entering by
the great gate of St. Dennis
Street, and taking the way
on the right hand.

THE INTRODUCTION.

ALTHOUGH that I, Nicholas Flammel, Notary, and abiding in Paris, in this year one thousand three hundred fourscore and nineteen, and dwelling in my house in the street of Notaries, near unto the Chapel of St. James of the Bouchery; although, I say, that I learned but a little Latin, because of the small means of my Parents, which nevertheless were, by them that envy me the most, accounted honest people; yet by the grace of God, and the intercession of the blessed Saints in Paradise of both sexes, and principally of St. James of Gallicia,

I have not wanted the understanding of the Books of the Philosophers, and in them learned their so-hidden secrets. And for this cause, there shall never be any moment of my life when I remember this high good, wherein upon my knees (if the place will give me leave), or otherwise, in my heart with all my affection, I shall not render thanks to this most benign God, which never suffereth the child of the just to beg from door to door, and deceiveth not them which wholly trust in his blessing.

Whilst, therefore, I Nicholas Flammel, Notary, after the decease of my Parents, got my living in our Art of Writing, by making Inventories, dressing accounts, and summing up the expenses of Tutors and Pupils, there fell into my hands for the sum of two florins, a guilded Book, very old and large. It was not of Paper, nor of Parchment, as other Books be, but was only made of delicate rinds (as it seemed unto me) of tender young trees. The cover of it was of brass, well bound, all engraven with letters, or strange figures; and for my part I think they might well be Greek Characters, or some-such-like ancient language. Sure I am, I could not read them, and I know well they were not notes nor letters of the Latin nor of the Gaul, for of them we understand a little. As for that which was within it, the leaves of bark or rind, were engraven, and with admirable diligence written, with a point of *Iron,* in fair and neat Latin letters, coloured. It contained thrice-seven leaves, for so were they counted in the top of the leaves, and always every seventh leaf was without any writing; but, instead thereof, upon the first seventh leaf, there was painted a *Rod* and *Serpents* swallowing it up. In the second seventh, a *Cross* where

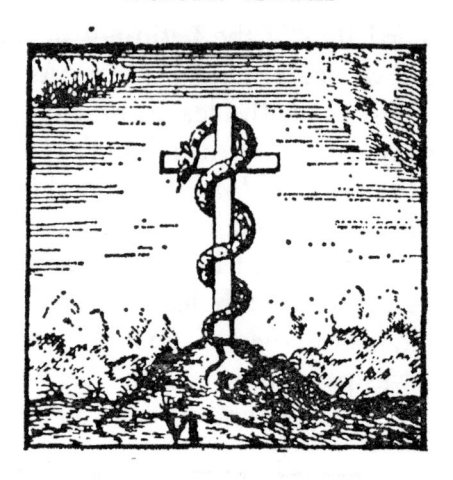

a *Serpent* was crucified; and in the last seventh there were painted Deserts, or Wildernesses, in the midst whereof ran many fair fountains, from whence there issued out a number of *Serpents*, which ran up and down here and there. Upon the first of the leaves was written in great Capital Letters of Gold: *Abraham the Jew, Prince, Priest, Levite, Astrologer, and Philosopher, to the Nation of the Jews, by the Wrath of God dispersed among the Gauls, sendeth Health.* After this it was filled with great execrations and curses (with this word *Maranatha,* which was often repeated there) against every person that should cast his eyes upon it if he were not Sacrificer or Scribe.

He that sold me this Book knew not what it was worth, no more than I when I bought it; I believe it had been stolen or taken from the miserable *Jews;* or found hid in some part of the ancient place of their abode. Within the Book, in the second leaf, he comforted his Nation, councelling them to fly vices, and above all, *Idolatry,* attending with sweet patience the coming of the *Messias,*

who should vanquish all the Kings of the Earth, and should reign with his people in glory eternally. Without doubt this had been some very wise and understanding man. In the third leaf, and in all the other writings that followed, to help his *Captive nation* to pay their *tributes* unto the *Roman Emperors,* and to do other things, which I will not speak of, he taught them in common words the *transmutation of Metals;* he painted the *Vessels* by the sides, and he advertised them of the *colours,* and of all the rest, saving of the *first Agent,* of the which he spake not a word; but only (as he said) in the fourth and fifth leaves entire he painted it, and figured it with very great cunning and workmanship: for although it was well and intelligibly figured and painted, yet no man could ever have been able to understand it without being well skilled in their *Cabala,* which goeth by tradition, and without having well studied their books. The fourth and fifth leaves therefore, were without any writing, all full of fair figures *enlightened,* or as it were *enlightened,* for the work was very exquisite. First, he painted a *young man* with wings at his ancles, having in his hand a *Caducean* rod, writhen about with two *Serpents,*

ALCHEMICAL HIEROGLYPHICS

wherewith he struck upon a helmet which covered his head. He seemed to my small judgment, to be the God *Mercury* of the *Pagans:* against him there came running and flying with open wings, a great old man, who upon his head had an *hourglass* fastened, and in his hand a hook (or sythe) like Death, with the which, in terrible and furious manner, he would have cut off the feet of *Mercury.* On the other side of the fourth leaf, he painted a fair *flower* on the top of a very high *mountain,* which was sore shaken with the *North wind;* it had the foot *blue,* the flowers *white* and *red,* the leaves shining like fine *gold:* and round about it the *Dragons* and *Griffons* of the *North* made their nests and abode. On the fifth leaf there was a fair *Rose-tree,* flowered in the midst of a sweet *Garden,* climbing up against a hollow *Oak;* at the foot whereof boiled a fountain of most *white water,* which ran head-long down into the depths, notwithstanding it first passed among the hands of infinite people, who digged in the earth seeking for it; but because they were blind, none of them knew it, except here and there one who considered the *weight.*

ALCHEMICAL HIEROGLYPHICS

On the last side of the fifth leaf there was a *King*, with a great *Fauchion*, who made to be killed in his presence by some *Soldiers* a great multitude of little *Infants*, whose Mothers wept at the feet of the unpitiful *Soldiers:* the blood of which Infants was afterwards by other Soldiers gathered up, and put in a great vessel, wherein the *Sun* and the *Moon* came to bathe themselves. And because that this History did represent the more part of that of the *Innocents* slain by *Herod*, and that in this Book I learned the greatest part of the *Art*, this was one of the causes why I placed

in their Church-yard these *Hieroglyphic Symbols* of this secret science. And thus you see that which was in the first five leaves. I will not represent unto you that which was written in good and intelligible Latin in all the other written leaves, for God would punish me; because I should commit a greater wickedness than he who (as it is said) wished that all the men of the World had but one head, that he might cut it off with one blow. Having with me, therefore, this *fair book,* I did nothing else day nor night but study upon it, understanding very well all the operations that it showed, but not knowing with what Matter I should begin, which made me very heavy and solitary, and caused me to fetch many a sigh. My wife *Perrenella,* whom I loved as myself, and had lately married, was much astonished at this, comforting me, and earnestly demanding if she could by any means deliver me from this trouble. I could not possibly hold my tongue, but told her all, and showed this *fair book,* whereof at the same instant that she saw it, she became as much enamoured as myself, taking extreme pleasure to behold the *fair cover, gravings, images,* and *portraits,* whereof, notwithstanding she understood as little as I; yet it was a great comfort to me to talk with her, and to entertain myself, what we should do to have the interpretation of them. In the end I caused to be painted within my *Lodging,* as naturally as I could, all the figures and portraits of the *fourth* and *fifth* leaf, which I showed to the greatest Clerks in *Paris,* who understood thereof no more than myself: I told them they were found in a Book that taught the *Philosophers' Stone,* but the greatest part of them made a mock both of me and that blessed *Stone,* excepting one called *Master Anselme,* who was a Licentiate in Physic, and studied hard in this *Science*. He had a great desire to have seen my Book, and there was nothing in the world he would not have done for a sight of it: but I always told him I had it not; only I made him a large description of the *Method*. He told me that the first portrait represented *Time,* which devoured all; and that according to the number of the *six* written leaves, there was required the space of six years, to perfect the *Stone;* and then, he said, we must turn the *glass,* and seethe it no more. And when I told him that this was not painted, but only to show and teach the first *Agent,* (as was said in the Book) he answered me that this decoction for *six* years space was, as it were, a *second Agent;* and that certainly the *first Agent* was there painted, which was the *white and heavy water,* which without doubt was *Argent Vive,* which they could not *fix,* nor cut off his *feet,* that is to say, take away his *volatility,* save by that long decoction in the purest blood of young Infants; for in that, this *Argent Vive* being joined with *gold* and *Silver,* was first turned with them into an *herb* like that which was there painted, and afterwards, by corruption, into *Serpents;* which *Serpents* being then wholly dried, and decocted by fire, were reduced into powder of *gold,* which should be the *Stone.* This was the cause that during the space of *one and twenty years,* I tried a thousand broulleryes, yet never with blood, for that was wicked and villaneous: for I found in my Book that the *Philosophers* called *Blood* the mineral spirit which is in the *Metals,* principally in the *Sun, Moon,* and *Mercury,* to the assembling whereof, I always tended; yet these interpretations for the most part were more subtil than true. Not seeing, therefore, in my works the *signs* at the time written in my Book, I was always to begin again. In the end, having lost all hope of ever understanding those *figures,* for my last refuge I made a vow to God and *St. James* of *Gallicia,* to demand the interpretation of them at some *Jewish Priest* in some *Synagogue* of *Spain:* whereupon, with the consent of *Perrenella,* carrying with me the *Extract* of the *Pictures,* having taken the *Pilgrims*' habit and staff, in the same fashion as you may see me without this same *Arch,* in the *Church-yard* in the which I put these *Hieroglyphical Figures,* where I have also set against the wall, on the one and the other side, a *Procession,* in which are represented by order all the colours of the *Stone,* so as they come and go, with this writing in French:—

> Much pleaseth God procession,
> If it be done in devotion.

Which is as it were the beginning of King *Hercules* his Book, which entreateth of the colours of the *Stone,* entitled *Iris,* or the *Rainbow,* in these termes, *The procession of the work is very pleasant unto Nature:* the which I have put there expressly for the great *Clerks* who shall understand the *Allusion.* In this same fashion, I say, I put myself upon my way; and so much I did that I arrived at *Montjoy,* and afterwards at *St. James,* where with great devotion I accomplished my vow. This done, in *Leon,* at my return, I met with a Merchant of *Bologn,* who made me known to a *Physician,* a *Jew* by Nation, and as then a *Christian,* dwelling in *Leon* aforesaid, who was very skilful in sublime Sciences, called Master *Canches.* As soon as I had shown him the figures of my Extract, he being ravished with great astonishment and joy, demanded of me incontinently if I could tell him any news of the *Book* from whence they were drawn? I answered him in *Latin,* (wherein he asked me the question) that I hoped to have some good news of the *Book,* if anybody could decipher unto me the *Enigmas.* All at that instant transported with great Ardor and joy, he began to dicipher unto me the beginning. But to be short, he well content to learn news where this Book should be, and I to hear him speak; and certainly he had heard much discourse of the Book, but, (as he said) as of a thing which was believed to be utterly lost, we resolved of our voyage, and from *Leon* we passed to *Oviedo,* and from thence to *Sansom,* where we put ourselves to Sea to come into *France.* Our voyage had been fortunate enough, and all-ready since we were entered into this Kingdom he had most truly interpreted unto me the greatest part of my figures, where even unto the very points and pricks he found great *mysteries,* which seemed unto me wonderful; when arriving at *Orleans,* this learned man fell extremely sick, being afflicted with excessive vomitings, which remained still with him of those he had suffered at Sea, and he was in such a continual fear of my forsaking him that he could imagine nothing like unto it. And although I was always by his side, yet would he incessantly call for me; but, in sum, he died at the end of the *seventh day* of his sickness, by reason whereof I was much grieved; yet, as well as I could, I caused him to be buried in the *Church* of the *Holy Cross* at *Orleans,* where he yet resteth: God have his soul, for he died a good *Christian.* And surely, if I be not hindered by death, I will give unto that *Church* some *revenue,* to cause some *Masses* to be said for his soul every day. He that would see the manner of my arrival and the joy of *Perrenella,* let him look upon us two, in this *City* of *Paris,* upon the door of the *Chapel* of *St. James* of the *Bouchery,* close by the one side of my *house,* where we are both painted, myself giving thanks at the feet of *St. James* of *Gallicia,* and *Perrenella* at the feet of *St. John,* whom she had so often called upon. So it was that by the grace of God, and the intercession of the happy and holy *Virgin,* and the blessed Saints *James* and *John,* I knew all that I desired, that is to say, The first *Principles,* yet not their first *preparation,* which is a thing most difficult above all the things in the world. But in the end I had that also, after long errors of *three years,* or thereabouts; during which time I did nothing but study and labour, so as you may see me without this *Arch,* where I have placed my *Processions* against the two Pillars of it, under the feet of *St. James and St. John,* praying always to God, with my Beads in my hand, reading attentively within a Book, and poysing the words of the Philosophers: and afterwards trying and proving the divers operations, which I imagined to myself by their only words. Finally, I found that which I desired, which I also soon knew by the strong *scent* and *odour* thereof. Having this, I easily accomplished the *Mastery,* for, knowing the *preparation* of the first *Agents,* and after following my Book according to the *letter,* I could not have missed it, though I would. Then, the first time that I made *projection* was upon *Mercury,* whereof I turned half-a-pound, or thereabouts, into pure *Silver,* better than that of the *Mine,* as I myself assayed, and made others assay many times. This was upon a Monday, the 17th of January, about noon, in my house, Perrenella only being present, in the year of the restoring of mankind, 1382. And afterwards, following always my Book, from word to word, I made *projection* of the *Red Stone* upon the like quantity of *Mercury,* in the presence likewise of Perrenella only, in the same house, the *five and twentieth day of April* following, the same year, about five *o'clock*

Ccc*

in the *evening;* which I transmuted truly into almost as much pure *Gold,* better assuredly than common Gold, more soft and more plyable. I may speak it with truth, I have made it three times, with the help of Perrenella, who understood it as well as I, because she helped in my operations, and without doubt, if she would have enterprised to have done it alone, she had attained to the end and perfection thereof. I had indeed enough when I had once done it, but I found exceeding great pleasure and delight in seeing and contemplating the *Admirable works of Nature* within the *Vessels.* To signify unto thee, then, how I have done it *three times,* thou shalt see in this *Arch,* if thou have any skill to know them, three *furnaces,* like unto them which serve for our *operations,* I was afraid a long time, that Perrenella could not hide the extreme joy of her felicity, which I measured by mine own, and lest she should let fall some word amongst her kindred of the great *treasures* which we possessed: for extreme *joy* takes away the understanding, as well as great *heaviness;* but the goodness of the most great God had not only filled me with this blessing, to give me a *wife* chaste and sage, for she was moreover, not only capable of reason, but also to do all that was reasonable, and more discrete and secret than ordinarily other women are. Above all, she was exceeding *devout,* and therefore, seeing herself without hope of children, and now well stricken in years, she began as I did, to think of God, and to give ourselves to the works of *Mercy.* At that time when I wrote this *Commentary,* in the year *one thousand four hundred and thirteen,* in the end of the year, after the decease of my faithful companion, which I shall lament all the days of my life; she and I had already founded, and endued with revenues, 14 *Hospitals* in this *City* of *Paris,* we had now built from the ground *three Chapels,* we had enriched with great gifts and good rents, *seven Churches,* with many reparations in their *Churchyards,* besides that which we have done at *Bologne,* which is not much less than that which we have done here. I will not speak of the good which both of us have done to particular poor folks, principally to *widows* and poor *orphans,* whose names if I should tell, and how I did it, besides that my reward should be given me in this World, I should likewise do displeasure to those good persons, whom I pray God bless, which I would not do for anything in the World. Building, therefore, these *Churches, Church-yards* and *Hospitals,* in this *City,* I resolved myself, to cause to be painted in the *fourth Arch* of the Church-yard of the *Innocents,* as you enter in by the great gate in *St. Dennis-street,* and taking the way on the right hand, the most true and essential marks of the *Art,* yet under veils, and *Hieroglyphical covertures,* in imitation of those which are in the guilded Book of *Abraham* the *Jew,* which may represent *two things,* according to the capacity and understanding of them that behold them: First, the *mysteries* of our future and undoubted *Resurrection,* at the day of Judgment, and coming of good *Jesus* (whom may it please to have mercy upon us), a History which is well agreeing to a *Church-yard.* And, secondly, they may signify to them, who are skilled in Natural *Philosophy,* all the principal and necessary operations of the *Mastery.* These *Hieroglyphic figures* shall serve as two ways to lead unto the heavenly life: the first and most open sense teaching the sacred *Mysteries* of our salvation; (as I will show hereafter) the other teaching every man that hath any small understanding in the *Stone* the lineary way of the work; which being perfected by any one, the change of evil into good takes away from him the root of all sin, (which is *covetousness*) making him liberal, gentle, pious, religious, and fearing God, how evil soever he was before, for from thenceforward he is continually ravished with the great grace and mercy which he hath obtained from God, and with the profoundness of his Divine and admirable works. These are the reasons which have moved me to set these forms in this fashion, and in this place, which is a *Church-yard,* to the end that if any man obtain this inestimable good, to conquer this *rich golden Fleece,* he may think with himself (as I did) not to keep the *talent* of *God* digged in the *Earth,* buying Lands and possessions, which are the vanities of this world: but rather to work charitably towards his brethren, rememebing himself that *he learned this secret amongst the bones of the dead,* in whose number he shall shortly be found; and that after this life he must render an account before a just and redoubtable *Judge,* who will censure even to an idle and vain word. Let him, therefore, who having well weighed my *words,* and well known and understood my *figures,* hath first gotten elsewhere the knowledge of the first *beginnings and Agents,* (for certainly in these *Figures* and *Commentaries* he shall not find any step or information thereof), perfect, to the glory of God, the *Mastery* of *Hermes,* remembering himself of the *Church Catholic, Apostolic,* and *Roman;* and of all other *Churches, Church-yards,* and *Hospitals;* and above all of the *Church* of the *Innocents* in this *City,* (in the *Church-yard* whereof he shall have contemplated these true demonstrations); opening bounteously his purse to them that are secretly poor honest people, desolate, weak women, widows, and forlorn orphans. So be it.

CHAPTER I.

Of the Theological Interpretations, which may be given to these Hieroglyphics, according to the sense of me, the Author.

I HAVE given to this *Church-yard* a *Charnel-house*, which is right over against this fourth *Arch*, in the midst of the *Church-yard*, and against one of the Pillars of this *Charnel-house* I have made be drawn with a coal, and grossly painted, *a man all black,* who looks straight upon these *Hieroglyphics,* about whom there is written in French; *I see a marvel, whereat I am much amazed.* This, as also three *plates* of *Iron* and *Copper* gilt, on the *East, West,* and *South* of the *Arch,* where these *Hieroglyphics* are, in the midst of the *Church-yard,* representing the holy *Passion* and *Resurrection* of the *Son* of *God;* this ought not to be otherwise interpreted than according to the common *Theological* sense, saving that this *black man* may as well proclaim it a wonder to see the admirable works of God in the *transmutation* of *Metals,* which is figured in these *Hieroglyphics,* which he so attentively looks upon, as to see buried so many *bodies,* which shall rise again out of their Tombs at the fearful day of *Judgment.* On the other part I do not think it needful to interpret in a *Theological* sense that *vessel* of *Earth* on the right hand of these figures, within the which there is a *Pen* and *Inkhorn,* or rather a vessel of *Philosophy,* if thou take away the *strings,* and join the *Penner* to the *Inkhorn:* nor the other two like it, which are on the two sides of the figures of *St. Peter* and *St. Paul,* within one of the which there is an N, which signifieth *Nicholas,* and within the other an F., which signifieth *Flammel.* For these vessels signify nothing else but that in the like of them, I have done the *Mastery* three times. Moreover he that will also believe that I have put these vessels in form of *Scutcheons,* to represent this *Pen* and *Inkhorn,* and the capital letters of my *name,* let him believe it if he will, because both these interpretations are true.

Neither must you interpret in a Theological sense that writing which followeth, in these terms;

"Nicholas Flammel, and Perrenella his wife," inasmuch as that signieth nothing but that I and my wife have given that *Arch.*

As to the third, fourth, and fifth Tables following, by the sides whereof is written, *"How the Innocents were killed by the command of King Herod,"* The *Theological* sense is well enough understood by the writing; we must only speak of the rest, which is above.

The two *Dragons* united together, the one within the other, of colour *black* and *blue* in a field of *sable,* that is to say, *black,* whereof the one hath the *wings* guilded, and the other hath none at all, are the *sins* which naturally are interchained, for the one hath his *original* and birth from another. Of them some may be easily *chased* away, as they *come* easily, for they fly towards us every hour; and those which have no *wings* can never be chased away, such as in the *sin* against the *holy Ghost.* The *gold* which is in the *wings* signifieth that the greatest part of sins cometh from the *unholy hunger* after *gold;* which makes so many people diligently to hearken from whence they may have it; and the colour *black* and *blue* showeth that these are the desires that come out of the dark pits of hell, which we ought wholly to fly from. These two *Dragons* may also morally represent unto us the Legions of *evil spirits* which are always about us, and which will accuse us before the just Judge, at the fearful day of Judgment; which do ask nor seek nothing else but to sift us.

The man and the woman which are next them, of an *orange colour,* upon a field *azure* and *blue,* signify that men and women ought not to have their hope in this World, for the *orange colour* intimates despair, or the letting-go of hope, as here; and the colour *azure* and *blue,* upon the which they are painted, shows us that we must think of heavenly things to come, and say as the rowl of the man doth, *"Man must come to the judgment of God;"* or as that of the woman, *"That day will be terrible indeed;"* to the end that keeping ourselves from the *Dragons,* which are *sins,* God may show mercy upon us.

Next after this, in a field of *Sinople,* that is *green,* are painted two men and one woman rising again, of the which one comes out of a *Sepulchre;* the other two out of the *Earth,* all three of colour exceeding *white* and *pure,* lifting their hands towards their eyes, and their eyes towards heaven on high. Above these three bodies there are two *Angels* sounding musical Instruments, as if they had called these dead to the day of judgment; for over these two *Angels* is the figure of our Lord *Jesus Christ,* holding the world in his hand, upon whose head an *Angel* setteth a Crown, assisted by two others, which say in their rowls, *"O Father Almighty, O good Jesus."* On the right side of this *Saviour* is painted *St. Paul,* clothed with *white* and *yellow,* with a Sword, at whose feet there is a man, clothed in a gown of *orange colour,* in which there appeared plaits or foulds of *black* and *white,* (which picture resembleth me to the life) and demandeth pardon of his sins, holding his hands joined together, from between which proceed these words, written in a rowl, *"Blot out the evils that I have done."* On the other side, on the left hand, is *St. Peter,* with his Key, clothed in *reddish-yellow,* holding his hand upon a woman clothed in a gown of *orange colour,* who is on her knees, representing to the life *Perrenella,* who holdeth her hands joined together, having a rowl where is written, *Christ, I beseech thee, be pitiful."* Behind whom there is an *Angel* on his knees, with a rowl, that saith, *"All hail thou Lord of*

Angels. There is also another Angel upon his knees, behind my Image, on the same side that *St. Paul* is on, which likewise holdeth a rowl, saying, *"O King everlasting."* All this is so clear, according to the explication of the *Resurrection* and future judgment, that it may easily be fitted thereto. So it seems this *Arch* was not painted for any other purpose but to represent this. And therefore we need not stay any longer upon it, considering that the least and most ignorant may well know how to give it this interpretation.

Next after the *three* that are rising again come two *Angels* more of an *Orange colour,* upon a *blue field,* saying on their rowls, *"Arise you dead, come to the Judgment of my Lord."* This also serves to the interpretaton of the *Resurrection.* As also the last figures, following which are, *A man, red vermillion,* upon a field of *Violet colour,* who holdeth the foot of a winged *Lion,* painted of *red vermillion* also, opening his throat, as it were to devour the *man:* For one may say that this is the figure of an unhappy sinner, who sleeping in a Lethargy of his corruption and vices, dieth without repentance and confession; who, without doubt, in this terrible Day shall be delivered to the *Devil*, here painted in form of a *red roaring Lion*, which will swallow and devour him.

CHAPTER II.

The Interpretations Philosophical, according to the Mastery of Hermes.

I DESIRE with all my heart that he who searcheth the secrets of the *Sages,* having in his *Spirit* passed over these *Ideas* of the life and resurrection to come, should, first, make his profit of them; and in the second place, that he be more advised than before, that he sound and search the depth of my *Figures, colours,* and *rowls;* principally of my *rowls,* because that in this Art they speak not vulgarly. Afterwards, let him ask of himself why the figure of *St. Paul* is on the right hand, in the place where the custom is to paint *St. Peter?* And on the other side that of *St. Peter,* in the place of the figure *St. Paul?* Why the figure of *St. Paul* is clothed in colours *white* and *yellow,* and that of *St. Peter* in *yellow* and *red?* Why also the *man* and the *woman,* who are at the feet of these two *Saints?* praying to *God,* as if it were the Day of *Judgment,* are apparelled in divers colours, and not naked, or else nothing else but bones, like them that are rising again? Why, in this *Day* of *Judgment,* they have painted this *man* and this *woman* at the feet of the *Saints?* for they ought to have been more low on *earth,* and not in *heaven.* Why also the two *Angels* in *Orange colours,* who say in their rowls, *"Arise you dead, come unto the Judgment of my Lord,* are clad in this colour, and out of their place, for they ought to be on high in heaven, with the two others, who play upon the *Instruments?* Why they have a field *Violet* and blue? but principally why their rowl, which speaks to the dead, ends in the open throat of the *red and flying Lion?* I would then, that after these, and many other questions which may justly be made, opening wide the eyes of his spirit, he come to conclude, that all this, not having been done without cause, there must be represented under this *barke* some great *secrets,* which he ought to pray *God* to discover unto him. Having than by degrees brought his belief to this pass, I wish also that he would further believe that these *figures* and *explications* are not made for them that have never seen the Books of the *Philosophers,* and who, not knowing the *Metallic* principles, cannot be named *Children* of this *Science;* for if they think to understand perfectly these *figures,* being ignorent of the *First Agent,* they will undoubtedly deceive themselves, and never be able to know anything at all. Let no man, therefore, blame me if he do not easily understand me, for he will be more blameworthy than I, inasmuch as not being initiated into these sacred and secret interpretations of the *first Agent,* (which is the *Key,* opening the gates of all *Sciences*) he would, notwithstanding, comprehend the most subtil conceptions of the *envious Philosophers,* which are not written but for them who already know these principles, which are never found in any book, because they leave them unto *God,* who revealeth them to whom he pleaseth, or else causeth them to be taught by the living voice of a *Master,* by Cabalistical tradition, which happeneth very seldom. Now then, *my Son,* let me so call thee, both because I am now come to a great age, and also for that, it may be, thou art otherwise a *child* of this *knowledge,* (*God* enable thee to learn, and after to work to his glory.) Hearken unto me, then, attentively, but pass no further if thou be ignorant of the aforesaid Principle.

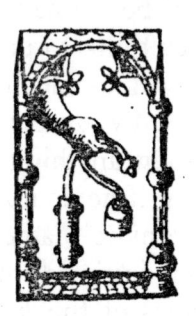

This *Vessel* of *earth* in this form is called by the *Philosophers* their *triple Vessel,* for within it there is, in the midst, a Stage, or floor, and upon that a dish or platter full of luke-warm ashes, within the which is set the *Philosophical Egg,* that is, a vial of glass full of *confections* of *Art,* (as of the scum of the *Red Sea,* and the fat of the *Mercurial* wind) which thou seest painted in form of a *Penner and Inkhorn.* Now this Vessel of *earth* is open above, to put in the *dish* and the *vial,* under which by the open gate, is put in the *Philosophical fire,* as thou knowest. So thou hast *three vessels;* and the threefold vessel, the envious have called an

Athanor, a *sieve, dung, Balneum Mariae,* a *Furnace,* a *Sphere,* the *green Lion, a prison, a grave, a urinal, a phial,* and a *Bolts head.* I myself in my *Summary,* or *Abridgement of Philosophy,* which I composed four years and two months past, in the end thereof named it the *house* and *habitation* of the *Poulet,* and the *ashes* of the Platter, the *chaff* of the Poulet. The common name is an *Oven,* which I should never have found if *Abraham* the *Jew* had not painted it, together with the fire proportionable, wherein consists a great part of the secret. For it is as it were the *belly,* or the *wombe,* containing the true natural heat to animate our *young King.* If this *fire* be not measured *(Clibanically,* saith *Calid the Persian, son of Jasichus;* if it be kindled with a sword, saith *Pythagoras;* if thou fire the Vessel, saith *Morien,* and makest it feel the heat of the fire, it will give thee a box on the ear, and burn his *flowers* before they be risen from the depth of his *marrow,* making them come out *red,* rather than *white,* and then thy work is spoiled; as also, if thou make too little fire, for then thou shalt never see the end, because of the *coldness* of the *natures,* which shall not have had motion sufficient to digest them together.

The heat, then, of thy *fire* in this *Vessel* shall be (as saith *Hermes* and *Rosinus*) according to the *Winter;* or rather, as saith *Diomedes,* according to the heat of a *bird,* which begins to fly so softly from the sign of *Aries* to that of *Cancer:* for know that the Infant at the beginning is full of *cold flegm,* and of *milk,* and that too vehement *heat* is an enemy of the *cold* and *moisture* of our *Embrion,* and that the two enemies, that is to say, our two elements of *cold* and *heat,* will never perfectly embrace one another but by little and little, having first long dwelt together, in the midst of the temperate heat of their *bath,* and being changed by long decoction into *sulphur incombustible.* Govern, therefore, sweetly with equality and proportion, thy proud and haughty natures, for lest if thou favour one more than another, they which naturally are enemies do grow angry against thee, through *jealousy* and dry choller, and make thee sigh for it a long time after. Besides this, thou must entertain them in this temperate heat perpetually, that is to say night and day, until the time that *Winter,* the time of *Moisture* of the matters, be passed, because they make their peace and join hands in being heated together;

whereas, should these natures find themselves but one only half-hour without *fire,* they would become for ever irreconcilable. See, therefore, the reason why it is said in the *Book of the seventy precepts, Look that their heat continue indefatigably without ceasing, and that none of their days be forgotten.* And *Kasis, the haste,* saith he, *that brings with it too much fire, is always followed by the Devil,* and error. *When the golden Bird,* saith *Diomedes, shall be come just to Cancer, and that from thence it shall run towards Libra, then thou mayest augment the fire a little. And in like manner, when this fair Bird shall fly from Libra towards Capricorn, which is the desired Autumn, the time of harvest, and of the fruits that are now ripe.*

CHAPTER III.

The two Dragons, of colour yellowish-blue, and black like the field.

LOOK well upon these *two Dragons*, for they are the true principles or beginnings of this *Philosophy*, which the *sages* have not dared to show to their own children. He which is undermost without wings, he is the *fixed* or the *male;* that which is uppermost is the *volatile*, or the *female, black and obscure,* which goes about to get the domination for many months. The first is called *Sulphur,* or heat and dryness; and the lattar *Argent-vive,* or cold and moisture; these are the *Sun* and the

Moon of the *Mercurial* source, and *sulphurous original,* which, by continual fire, are adorned with *royal* habilaments; that, being united and afterwards changed into a *quintessence,* they may overcome everything *Metallic,* how solid, hard and strong soever it be. These are the *Serpents* and *Dragons* which the ancient *Egyptians* have painted in a *Circle,* the *head* biting the *tail,* to signify that they proceed from one and the same thing, and that it alone was sufficient, and that in the turning and *circulation* thereof it made itself perfect. These are the *Dragons,* which the ancient Poets have feigned did without sleeping keep and watch the Golden Apples of the Gardens of the Virgins *Hesperides.* These are they upon whom *Jason,* in his adventure for the Golden Fleece, poured the broth or liquor prepared by the fair *Medea;* of the discourse of whom the Books of the *Philosophers* are so full, that there is no *Philosopher* that ever was but he hath written of it, from the time of the truth telling *Hermes, Trismegistus, Orpheus, Pythagorus, Artephius, Morienus,* and the other following, even unto myself. These are the *two Serpents,* given and sent by *Juno* (that is, the nature Metallic) the which the strong *Hercules,* (that is to say, the sage and wise man) must *strangle* in his *cradle;* that is, overcome and kill them, to make them putrify, corrupt and engender at the beginning of his work. These are the *two Serpents* wrapped and twisted about the *Caduceus,* or *rod* of *Mercury,* with the which he exerciseth his great power, and transformeth himself as he listeth. He, saith *Haly,* that shall kill the one, shall also kill the other, because the one cannot die but with his brother. These two men, (which *Avicen* calleth the *Corussene bitch* and the *Armenian dog,*) these two, I say, being put together in the vessel of the *Sepulchre,* do bite one another cruelly, and by their great poison and furious rage they never leave one another from the moment that they have seized on one another (if the *cold* hinder them not) till both of them by their slavouring venom and mortal hurts be all of a gore-blood, over all the parts of their bodies, and finally, killing one another, be stewed in their proper *venom,* which after their death, changeth them into living and *permanent water;* before which time, they loose in their corruption and putrefaction their first natural forms, to take afterwards one only new, more noble and better form. These are the two *Sperms,* which is turned into this *Earth, black* of the *black* most *black,* wholly to accomplish this peace: for the *Earth,* which is *cold* and *dry,* finding himself of kindred and alliance with the *dry* and *moist,* which are enemies, will wholly appease and accord them. Dost thou not then consider a most perfect mixture of all the four *Elements,* having first turned them into *water,* and now into *Earth!* I will also teach thee hereafter the other conversions; into *air,* when it shall be all *white;* and into *fire,* when it shall be of a most perfect *purple.* Then thou hast here two *natures* married together, whereof the one hath conceived by the other and by this *conception* it is turned into the body of the *Male,* and the *Male* into that of the *Female;* that is to say, they are made one only body, which is the *Androgyne,* or *Hermaphrodite* of the *Ancients,* which they have also called otherwise, *the head of the Crow,* or *natures converted.* In this fashion I paint them here, because thou hast two natures reconciled, which (if they be guided and governed wisely) can form an *Embrion* in the womb of the *Vessel,* and afterwards bring forth a most puissant *King,* invincible and incorruptible, because it will be an admirable *quintessence.* Thus they should see in the air a venomous fume and a stinking, worse in flame and in poison than the envenomed head of a *Serpent* and *Babylonian Dragon*. The cause why I have painted these two *sperms* in the form of *Dragons* is because their stink is exceedingly great, and like the stink of them, and the *exhalations* which arise within the glass are dark *black, blue,* and *yellowish,* (like as these two *Dragons* are painted) the force of which, and of the *bodies* dissolved, is so venomous, that truly there is not in the world a ranker *poison;* for it is able by the force and stench thereof to mortify and kill every thing living. The *Philosopher* never feels this *stench* if he break not his vessels, but only he judgeth it to be such by the sight, and the changing of *colours,* proceeding from the rottenness of his confections.

These colours signify the *putrefaction* and *generation* which is given us, by the biting and dissolution of our *perfect bodies,* which dissolution proceedeth from external heat aiding, and from the *Pontique fieriness,* and admirable sharp virtue of the poison of our *Mercury,* which maketh and resolveth into a pure cloud, that is, into impalpable powder, all that which it finds to resist it. So the heat working upon and against the *radical metallic viscous,* or *oily* moisture, engendereth upon the subject *blackness*. For, at the same time, the Matter is dissolved, is corrupted, groweth black, and conceiveth to engender; for all *corruption is generation,* and therefore ought *blackness* to be much desired; for that is the *black sail* with which the *Ship of Theseus* came back victorious from *Crete,* which was the cause of the death of his *Father,* so must this father die, to the intent that from the ashes of this *Phoenix* another may spring, and that the *son* may be *King.* Assuredly, he that seeth not this *blackness* at the beginning of his operations, during the days of the *Stone,* what other colour soever he see, he shall altogether fail in the *Mastery,* and can do no more with that *Chaos:* for he works not well if he *putrify* not; because if he do not *putrify* he doth not *corrupt,* nor *engender,* and by consequent, the *Stone* cannot take *vegetative* life to increase and multiply. And in all truth, I tell thee again, that though thou work upon the true matter, if at the beginning, after thou hast put thy *Confections* in the *Philosophic Egg,* that is to say, some time after the fire has stirred them up, if then I say, thou seest not this *head of the Crow,* the black of the *blackest black,* thou must begin again, for this fault is irreparable, and not to be amended; especially the *Orange-colour,* or *half-red,* is to be feared; for if at the beginning thou see that in thine *Egg,* without doubt thou burnest, or hast burnt the *verdure* and liveliness of thy *Stone.* The colour which thou must have ought to be entirely perfected in *blackness,* like to that of these *Dragons,* in the space of *forty days.* Let them, therefore, which shall not have these essential marks, retire themselves betimes from their operations, that they may redeem themselves from assured loss. Know also, and note it well, that in this Art it is but nothing to have this *blackness,* there is nothing more easy to come by: for from almost all things in the world, mixed with *moisture,* thou mayest have a *blackness* by the fire; but thou must have a *blackness* which comes of the perfect *Metallic bodies,* which lasts a long space of time, and is not destroyed in less than *five months,* after the which followeth immediately the desired *whiteness.* If thou hast this, thou hast enough, but not all. As for the colour *blueish* and *yellowish,* that signifieth that *Solution* and *Putrefaction* is not yet finished, and that the colours of our *Mercury* are not as yet well mingled, and rotten with the rest. Then, this *blackness*, and these colours, teach plainly, that in this beginning the matter and compound, begins to rot and dissolve into powder, less than the *Atoms* of the *Sun*, the which afterwards are changed into *coator permanent*. And this dissolution is by the envious *Philosophers* called *Death, Destruction,* and *Perdition,* because that the *natures* change their *form,* and from hence are proceeded so many *Allegories* of *dead men, tombs,* and *sepulchres.* Others have called it *Calcination, Deundation, Separation, Trituration,* and *Assation,* because the Confections are changed and reduced into most small pieces and parts. Others have called it *Reduction into the first matter, Mollification, Extraction, Commixtion, Liquifaction, Conversion of Elements, Subtiliation, Division, Humation, Impastation,* and *Distillation,* because that the *Confections* are melted, brought back into seed, softened, and circulated within the glass. Others have called it *Xir,* or *Iris, Putrefaction, Corruption, Cymmerian darkness, a gulph, Hell, Dragons, Generation, Ingression, Submersion, Complection, Conjunction,* and *Impregation,* because that the matter is black and waterish, and that the natures are perfectly mingled, and hold one of another. For when the heat of the Sun worketh upon them, they are changed, first into *powder,* or fat and glutinous *water,* which feeling the heat, flieth on high to the *Poulets'* head, with the *smoke,* that is to say, with the wind and air; from thence this water melted, and drawn out of the *Confections,* goeth down again, and in descending reduceth and dissolveth, as much as it can, the rest of the *Aromatical Confections,* always doing so until the whole be like a black broth somewhat fat. Now you see why they call this *Sublimation* and *Volatization,* because it flieth on high; and *Ascension* and *Decension,* because it mounteth and descendeth within the glass. A while after the water beginneth to *thicken* and *coagulate* somewhat more, growing very *black,* like unto pitch, and finally comes the *Body* and *earth* which the envious have called *Terra-foetida,* that is, *stinking-earth:* for then, because of the perfect *putrefaction,* which is as natural as any other can be, this earth stinks, and gives a smell like the odour of *graves* filled with rottenness, and with bodies as yet charged with their natural moisture. This *earth* was by *Hermes* called

Terra foliata, or the *Earth of leaves;* yet his true and proper name is *Leton,* which must afterward be *whitened.* The Ancient Sages that were *Cabalists* have described it in their *Metamorphoses* under the History of the Serpent of *Mars,* which had devoured the companions of *Cadmus,* who show him piercing him with his lance against a *hollow Oak.* Note this Oak.

CHAPTER IV.

Of the man and the woman clothed in a gown of Orange colour, upon a field azure and blue, and of their rowls.

THE *man* painted here doth expressly resemble *myself* to the natural, as the *woman* doth lively figure *Perrenella*. The cause why we are painted to the life is not particular to this purpose, for it needed but to represent a *male* and a *female,* to the which our two particular resemblance was not necessarily required, but it pleased the *painter* to put us there, just as he hath done higher in this *Arch,* at the feet of the Figure of Saint *Paul* and Saint *Peter,* according to that we were in our youth; as he hath likewise done in other places, as over the *door* of the *Chapel* of Saint *James* in the *Bouchery* near to my house, (although that for this last there was a particular cause) as also over the door of *Saincte Geneuiefue de's Ardans*, where thou mayest see me. I made then to be painted here two *bodies*, one of a *Male* and another of a *Female*, to teach thee that in this second operation thou hast truly, but yet not perfectly, two *natures*, conjoined and married together, the *Masculine* and the *Feminine;* or rather the four *Elements;* and that the four natural enemies, the *hot* and *cold, dry* and *moist,* begin to approach amiably one towards another, and by means of the *Mediators* and Peacemakers, lay down by little and little, the ancient enmity of the old *Chaos.* Thou knowest well enough who these *Mediators* and Peace-makers are; between the *hot* and the *cold* there is *moisture,* for he is kinsman and allied to them both; to *hot* by his *heat,* and to *cold* by his *moisture.* And this is the reason why to begin to make this peace, thou hast already, in the precedent operation, converted all the *Confections* into *water* by *dissolution.* And afterwards thou hast made to *coagulate* the *water, masculine* and *feminine,* described at the begining of my *Abridgment of Philosophy,* which are engendered (say *Kasis, Avicen,* and *Abraham* the *Jew*) within the reins and entrails, and of the operations of the four *Elements.* These are the radical moisture of Metals, *Sulphur* and *Argent vive,* not vulgar, and such as are sold by the Merchants and Apothecaries, but those which give us those two fair and dear bodies which we love so much. These two sperms, saith *Democritus,* are not found upon the *earth* of the *living;* the same saith *Avicen,* but he addeth, that they gather them from the dung, odour and rottenness of the *Sun* and *Moon.* O, happy are they that know how to gather them, for of them they afterwards make a *treacle,* which hath power over all grief, maladies, sorrows, infirmities, and weaknesses, and which fighteth puissantly against *death,* lengthening the life, according to the permission of *God,* even to the time determined, triumphing over the miseries of this world, and filling a man with the riches thereof. Of these two *Dragons* or Principles *Metallic,* I have said in my forealledged *Summary,* that the Enemy would by his heat inflame his enemy, and that then if they take not heed, thou seest the principal and most necessary reason of this representation. The second cause, (which is also well to be noted) was because I must of necessity paint *two bodies,* because in this operation it behoveth that thou *divide* that which hath been *coagulated,* to give afterwards *nourishment,* which is *milk* of *life,* to the little Infant when it is born, which is endued (by the living God) with a *vegetable soul.*

This is a secret most admirable and secret, which, for want of understanding, it hath made fools of all those that have sought it without finding it; and hath made every man wise that beholds it with the eyes of his *body,* or of his *spirit.*

Thou must then make two parts and portions of this *Coagulated body;* the one of which shall serve for *Azoth,* to wash and cleanse the other, which is called *Leton,* which must be whitened. He which is washed is the *Serpent Python,* which (having taken his being from the corruption of the slime of the *Earth* gathered together by the waters of the *deluge,* when all the confections were water) must be killed and overcome by the arrows of the *God Apollo,* by the *yellow Sun,* that is to say, by *our fire,* equal to that of the *Sun.*

He which *washeth,* or rather the *washings,* which must be continued with the other moiety, these are the *teeth* of that *Serpent* which the sage workman, the valiant *Thesus,* will sow in the same *Earth,* from whence there shall spring up armed *Soldiers,* which shall in the end discomfit themselves, suffering themselves by opposition to resolve into the same nature of the *Earth,* and the workman to bear away his deserved conquests. It is of this that the *Philosophers* have written so often, and so often repeated it: *It dissolves itself, it congeals itself, it makes itself black, it makes itself white, it kills itself, and it quickens itself.* I have made their field be painted *azure* and *blue,* to show that I do but now begin to get out from the most *black blackness;* for the *azure* and *blue* is one of the first colours that the *dark woman* lets us see; that is to say, *moisture* giving place a little to *heat* and *dryness.* The *man* and *woman* are almost all *orange-coloured,* to show that our *Bodies* (or our *body,* which the wise men here call *Rebis*) hath not as yet *digestion* enough, and that the *moisture* from whence comes the *black, blue* and *azure,* is but half vanquished by the *dryness.*

For when *dryness* bears rule all will be *white;* and when it fighteth with, or is equal to the *moisture,* all will be in part according to these present colours. The envious have also called these *confections* in this operation, *Nummus, Ethelia, Arena, Boritis, Corsufle, Cambar, Albaraeris, Duenech, Randeric, Kuhul, Thabricis Ebisemech, Ixir,* etc., which they have commanded to make *white.*

The *woman* hath a *white* circle in form of a *rowl* round about her body, to show thee that *Rebis* will begin to come white in that very fashion, beginning first at the *extremities,* round about this white *circle. Scala Phylosophorum,* i.e., the Book entitled *The Philosophers' Ladder,* saith thus, *The sign of the first perfect whiteness is the manifestation of a certain little circle of hair, that is passing over the head, which will appear on the sides of the vessels round about the matter in a kind of a cierine or yellowish colour.*

There is written in their Rowls, *"Man shall come to the Judgment of God." Vere,* (saith the woman) *"Truly that will be a terrible day."* These are not passages of holy *Scripture,* but only sayings which speak, according to the *Theological* sense, of the *Judgment* to come; I have put them there to serve myself of them towards him that beholds only the gross outward and most natural *Artifice,* taking the interpretation thereof to concern only the *Resurrection;* and also it may serve for them, that gathering together the *Parables* of the *Science,* take to them the eyes of *Lynecous,* to pierce deeper than the *visible objects.* There is then, *Man shall come to the Judgment of God: Certainly that day shall be terrible.* That is as if I should have said: It behoves that this come to the colour of *perfection,* to be judged and cleansed from all his *blackness* and filth, and be *spiritualized* and *whitened. Surely that day will be terrible,* yet certainly as you shall find in the *Allegory of Aristeus,* Horror holds us in prison by the space of *fourscore days,* in the darkness of the *waters,* in the extreme heat of the *Summer,* and in the troubles of the *Sea.* All which things ought first to pass before our *King* can become *white,* coming from death to life, to overcome afterwards all his enemies. To make thee understand yet somewhat better this *Albification,* which is harder and more difficult than all the rest, (for till that time thou mayest err at every step, but afterwards thou canst not, except thou break thy *vessels*) I have also made for thee this Table following.

CHAPTER V.

The figure of a man like that of Saint Paul, clothed with a robe white and yellow, bordered with gold, holding a naked Sword, having at his feet a man on his knees, clad in a robe of orange colour, black and white, holding a rowl.

MARK well this *man* in the form of *Saint Paul*, clothed in a robe entirely of a *yellowish white*. If thou consider him well, he turns his body in such a *posture* as shows that he would take the *naked Sword*, either to cut off the *head* or to do some other thing to that *man* which is on his knees at his feet, clothed in a robe of *orange colour, white* and *black,* which saith in his rowl, *Blot out all the evil that I have done;* as if he should say, *Take away from me my blackness;* A term of Art: for *Evil* signifieth in the *Allegory Blackness,* as it is often found in *Turba Philosophorum: Seethe it until it come to blackness, which will be*

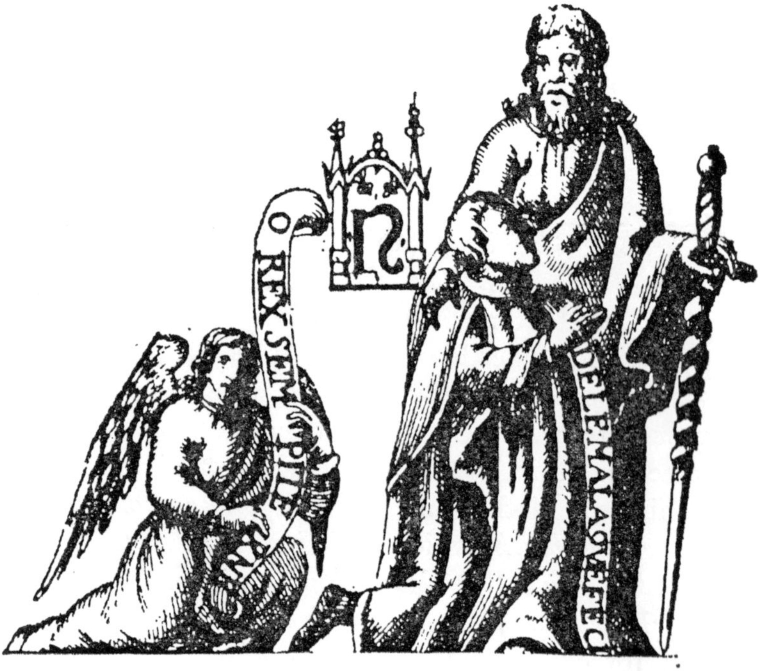
O REX SEMPITE
DELE MALA QVE FEC

thought Evil. But wouldst thou know what is meant by this *man* that taketh the *Sword?* It signifies that thou must cut off the head of the *Crow,* that is to say, of the man clothed in divers *Colours,* who is on his knees. I have taken this portrait and figure out of *Hermes Trismegistus,* in his Book of the *Secret Art,* where he saith, *Take away the head of this black man, cut off the head of the Crow:* that is to say, *Whiten our black.* Lambs-springk, that noble *German,* hath also used it in the *Commentary* of his *Hieroglyphics,* saying, *In this wood there is a Beast all covered with black; if any man cut off his head he will lose his blackness, and put on a most white colour. Will you understand what that is? The blackness is called the head of the Crow, the which being taken away, at the instant comes the white colour. Then that is to say, when the Cloud appears no more, this body is said to be without a head.* These are his proper words. In the same sense, the *Sages* have also said in other places, *Take the Viper which is called De rexa, cut off his head etc;* that is to say, take away from him his *blackness.* They have also used this *Periphrasis,* when to signify the multiplication of the *Stone,* they have feigned a

E

Serpent Hydra, whereof if one cut off one head, there will spring in the place thereof ten; for the stone augments tenfold, every time that they cut off this *head of the Crow,* that they make it *black,* and afterwards *white;* that is to say, that they dissolve it anew, and afterward *coagulate* it again.

Mark how this naked Sword is wreathed about with a *black girdle,* and that the ends thereof are not so wreathed at all. This naked shining *Sword* is the stone for the *white,* or the white stone, so often by the *Philosophers* described under this form. To come then, to this perfect and sparkling *whiteness,* thou must understand the wreathings of this black girdle, and follow that which they teach, which is the quantity of the imbibitions. The two ends which are not wreathed about at all represent the beginning and the ending: for the beginning, it teacheth that you must *imbibe* it at the first time gently and scarcely, giving it then a little milk, as to a little *Child* newborn, to the intent that *Isir* (as the *Authors* say) be not drowned. The like must we do at the end, when we see that our *King* is *full,* and will have no more. The middle of these operations is painted by the five whole *wreathes,* or *rounds,* of the *black girdle,* at what time (because our *Salamander* lives of the *fire,* and in the midst of the *fire,* and indeed is a *fire,* and an *Ardent vive,* or quicksilver, that runs in the midst of the *fire,* fearing nothing) thou must give him abundantly, in such sort that the *Virgin's milk* compass all the matter round about.

I have made to be painted black all these *wreathes,* or rounds of the girdle, because these are the *imbibitions,* and by consequent, *blackness;* for the *fire* with the *moisture* (as it hath been often said) causeth *blackness.* And as these *five* whole *wreathes,* or rounds, show that you must do this *five times* wholly, so likewise they let you know that you must do this in *five* whole months, a month to every *imbibition.* See here the reason why *Haly Abenraged* said, *The Coction or boiling of the things is done in three times fifty days.* It is true that if thou count these little imbibitions at the beginning and at the end there are seven. Whereupon one of the most envious hath said, *Our head of the Crow is leprous, and therefore he that would cleanse it, he must make it go down seven times into the River of regeneration of Jordan, as the Prophet commanded the leprous Naaman the Syrian.* Comprehending herein the beginning, which is but a few days, the middle and the end, which is also very short. I have then given thee this Table, to tell thee that thou must *whiten* my body, which is upon the knees; and demandeth no other thing: for Nature always tends to perfection, which thou shalt accomplish by the apposition of *Virgin's milk,* and by the decoction of the matters which thou shalt make with this *milk,* which being dried upon this body will colour it into this same *white yellow,* which he who takes the *Sword* is clothed withal, in which colour thou must make thy *Corsufle* to come. The vestments of the figure of *Saint Paul* are bordered largely with a *golden* and *red citrine* colour. O my Son, praise God, if ever thou seest this, for now hast thou obtained mercy from Heaven: *Imbibe* it then, and tein it till such time as the little Infant be hardy and strong, to combat against the *water* and the fire. In accomplishing the which, thou shalt do that which *Demagoras, Senior,* and *Hali* have called, *The putting of the Mother into the Infants' belly, which Infant the Mother had but lately brought forth:* for they call the *Mother* the *Mercury of Philosophers,* wherewith they make their imbibitions and fermentations, and the *Infant* they call the *Body,* to tein or colour the which this *Mercury* is gone out. Therefore I have given thee these two figures, to signify the *Albification;* for in this place it is that thou hast need of great help, for here all the World is deceived. This operation is indeed *a labyrinth,* for here there present themselves a thousand ways at the same instant, besides that, thou must go to the *end* of it, directly contrary to the *beginning,* in *coagulating* that which before thou *dissolvest,* and in making *earth* that which before thou madest *water.* When thou hast made it *white,* then hast thou overcome the *enchanted Bulls,* that cast fire and smoke out of their nostrils. *Hercules* hath cleansed the *stable* full of odour, of rottenness, and of *blackness. Jason* hath poured the decoction or broth upon the *Dragons of Colchos,* and thou hast in thy power the horn of *Amalthaea,* which (although it be *white*) may fill thee all the rest of thy life with glory, honor, and riches. To have the which, it hath behoved thee to fight valiantly, and in manner of an *Hercules;* for this *Achelous,* this moist river, is endued with a most mighty force, besides that he often transfigures himself from one form to another. Thus hast thou done all, because the rest is without difficulty. These transfigurations are particularly described in the *Book of the Seven Egyptian Seals,* where it is said (as also by all Authors,) that the *Stone, before it will wholly forsake his blackness, and become white in the fashion of a most shining marble, and of a naked flaming sword, will put on all the colours that thou canst possibly imagine; often will it melt, and often coagulate itself, and amidst these divers and contrary operations (which the vegetable-soul that is in it makes it perform at one and the same time,) it will grow Citrine, green, red (but not of a true red,) it will become yellow, blue and orange colour, until that, being wholly overcome by dryness and heat, all these infinite colours will end in this admirable Citrine whiteness,* of the colour of Saint *Pauls'* garments, which in a short time will become like the colour of the naked *sword;* afterwards by the means of a more strong and long decoction, it will take in the end a *red Citrine* colour, and afterward the perfect *red* of the *vermillion,* where it will repose itself for ever. I will not forget, by the way, to advertise thee that the Milk of the *Moon* is not as the *Virgin's milk* of the *Sun;* think then that the *imbibitions* of *whiteness* require a more *white milk* than those of a *golden redness;* for in this passage I had thought I should have missed, and so I had done indeed had it not been for *Abraham the Jew;* for this reason I have made to be painted for thee the Figure which taketh the naked sword, in the colour which is necessary for thee; for it is the Figure of that which whiteneth.

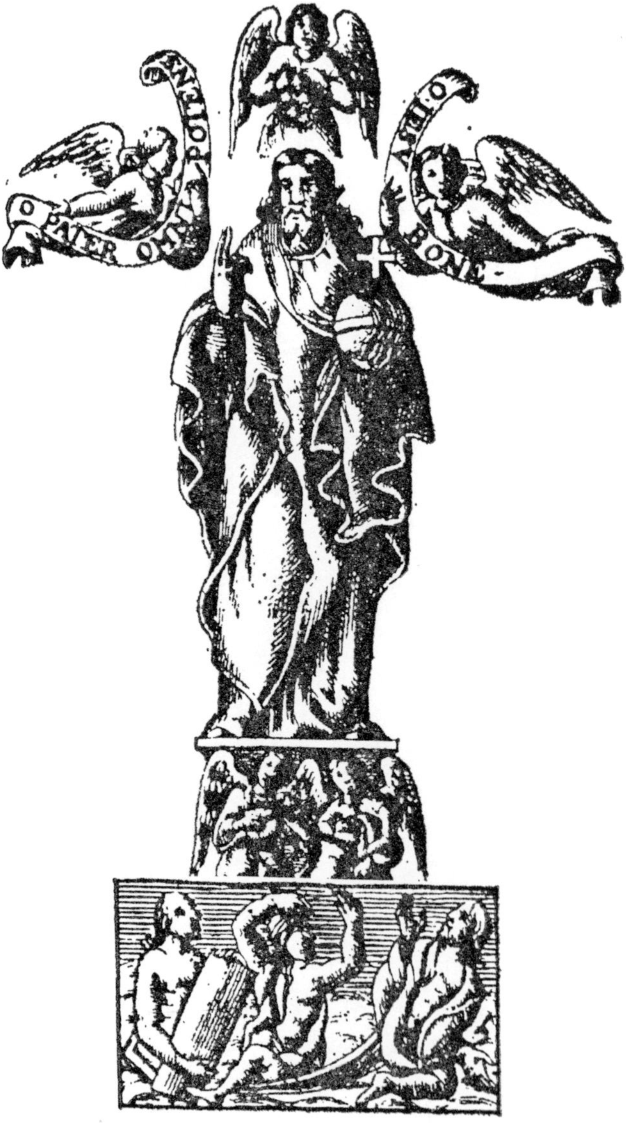
O PATER OMNIPOTENS
BONE

CHAPTER VI.

Upon a green field, three resuscitants, or which rise again, two men and one woman, altogether white: Two Angels beneath, and over the Angels the figure of our Saviour coming to Judge the world, clothed with a robe which is perfectly Citrine white.

I HAVE so made to be painted for thee a field *vert*, because that in this decoction the confections become *green*, and keep this colour longer than any other after the *black*. This *greenness* shows particularly that our *Stone* hath a vegetable soul, and that by the Industry of *Art* it is turned into a true and pure *tree*, to bud abundantly, and afterwards to bring forth infinite little sprigs and branches. O *happy green* (saith the *Rosary*) *which dost produce all things; without thee nothing can increase, vegetate, nor multiply.* The three *folk* rising again, clothed in *sparkling white,* represent the *Body, Soul,* and *Spirit* of our *white Stone.* The

Philosophers do ordinarily use these terms of *Art* to hide the secret from evil men. They call the *Body* that *black earth,* obscure and dark, which we make *white.* They call the *Soul* the other half divided from the *Body,* which by the will of God and power of nature, gives to the *body* by his imbibitions and fermentations a vegetable soul, that is to say, power and virtue to bud, increase, multiply and become white, as a naked shining sword. They call the *Spirit* the *tincture* and *dryness;* which as a Spirit hath power to pierce all *Metallic* things. I should be too tedious if I should show thee how good reason they had to say always and in all places, *Our Stone hath semblably to a man, a Body, Soul,* and *Spirit.* I would only that thou note well, that as a man endued with a *Body, Soul,* and *Spirit,* is notwithstanding but one; so likewise thou hast now but one only white confection, in the which nevertheless there are a *Body,* a *Soul,* and a *Spirit,* which are inseparably united. I could easily give very clear comparisons and expositions of this *Body, Soul,* and *Spirit;* but to explicate them, I must of necessity speak things which God reserves to reveal unto them that fear and love him, and consequently ought not to be written. I have then made to be painted here a *Body*, a *Soul, and a Spirit*, all *white*, as if they were rising again, to show thee, that the *Sun* and *Moon*, and *Mercury*, are raised again in this operation; that is to say, are made *Elements* of air, and whitened: for we have heretofore called the *Blackness Death*; and so, continuing the *Metaphor*, we may call *Whiteness Life;* which cometh not but with and by a *Resurrection*. The *Body*, to show this more plainly, I have made to be painted lifting up the stone of his tomb, wherein it was inclosed. The *Soul*, because it cannot be put into the *earth,* it comes not out of a *tomb,* but only I have made it be painted amongst the *Tombs,* seeking its body, in form of a *woman,* having her hair dishevelled. The *Spirit* which likewise cannot be put into a grave, I have made to be painted in fashion of a man coming out of the *earth,* not from a Tomb. They are all *white;* so the *blackness,* that is, *death* is vanquished, and they, being whitened, are from henceforward incorruptible. Now lift up thine eyes on high, and see our *King* coming, crowned and raised again, which hath overcome *Death,* the darkness and moistures; behold him in the form wherein our *Saviour* shall come, who shall eternally unite unto him all pure and clean souls, and will drive away all impurity and uncleanness, as being unworthy to be united to his *divine Body*. So by comparison (but first asking leave of the *Catholic, Apostolic,* and *Roman Church,* to speak in this manner, and praying every debonaire soul to permit me to use this similitude) see here our white *Elixir,* which from henceforward will inseparably unite unto himself every pure *Metallic* nature, changing it into his own most fine *silvery* nature, rejecting all that is impure, strange, *Heterogeneal,* or of another kind. Blessed be God, who of his goodness gives us grace to be able to consider this sparkling white, more perfect and shining than any compound nature, and more noble next after the *immortal soul,* than any substance having life, or not having life; for it is a *quintessence,* a most pure *silver,* that hath passed the *Coppel,* and *is seven times refined,* saith the royal Prophet *David.*

It is not needful to interpret what the two *Angels* signify, who play on Instruments over the heads of them who are raised again. These are rather divine spirits, singing the marvels of *God,* in this miraculous operation, than Angels who call to judgment. To make an express difference between these and them, I have given the one of them a *Lute,* the other a *haultboy,* but none of them *trumpets,* which yet are wont to be given to them who are to call us to *Judgment.* The like may be said of the three Angels who are over the head of our *Saviour,* whereof the one crowneth him, and the other two assisting, say in their rowls, *O Almighty Father, O good Jesus;* in rendering unto him eternal thanks.

CHAPTER VII.

Upon a field violet and blue, two Angels of an orange colour, and their rowls.

THIS violet and blue field showeth that, being to pass from the *white stone* to the *red*, thou must imbibe it with a little *virgin's milk* of the *Sun*, and that these colours come out of the *Mercurial* moisture which thou hast dried upon the *Stone*. In this operation of rubifying, although thou do *imbibe* thou shalt not have much *black*, but of *violet*, *blue*, and of the colour of the *Peacocks' tail*. For our *stone* is so triumphant in *dryness*, that as soon as thy *Mercury* toucheth it the nature thereof rejoicing in his like nature, it is joined unto it, and drinketh it greedily, and therefore the black that comes of moisture can show itself but a little, and that under these colours *violet* and *blue,* because that *dryness* (as it is said) doth by-and-by govern absolutely. I have also made to be painted for thee these two *Angels* with wings, to represent unto thee the two substances of thy confections, the *Mercurial* and the *sulphurous* substance, the *fixed* as well as the *volatile,* being perfectly fixed together, do also fly together within thy vessel: for in this operation the fixed body will generally mount to heaven, being all *spiritual,* and from thence it will descend unto the *earth,* and whithersoever thou wilt, following every where the *spirit,* which is alway moved upon the *fire.* Inasmuch as they are made one selfsame nature, and the compound is all *spiritual,* and the *spiritual all corporal,* so much hath it been subtilized upon *our Marble,* by the precedent operations. The natures, then, are here transmuted into *Angels;* that is to say, are made *spiritual* and most subtil, so are they now the true *tinctures.* Now remember thee to begin the *rubifying* by the opposition of *Mercury Citrine red;* but thou must not pour on much, and only once or twice, according as thou shalt see occasion; for this operation ought to be done by a *dry fire,* and by a *dry sublimation,* and *calcination.* And truly I tell thee here a secret which thou shalt very seldom find written, so far am I from being envious, that would to God every man knew how to make *gold* to his own will, that they might live, and lead forth to pasture their fair flocks, without Usury or going to law, in imitation of the holy *Patriarchs,* using only (as our first Fathers did) to exchange one thing for another; and yet to have that they must labour as well as now. Howbeit, for fear to offend *God,* and to be the instrument of such a change, which peradventure would prove evil, I must take heed to represent or write where it is that we hide the *keys* which can open all the doors of the secrets of nature, or to open or cast up the *earth,* in that place contenting myself to show the things which will teach every one to whom *God* shall give permission to know, what property the sign of the *Balance* or *Libra* hath, when it is enlightened by the *Sun* and *Mercury* in the month of *October.* These *Angels* are painted of an *orange colour* to let thee know that thy white confections have been a little more digested, or boiled, and that the *black* of the *violet* and *blue* hath been already chased away by the *fire:* for this *orange colour* is compounded of the fair *golden Citrine red* (which thou hast so long waited for) and of the remainder of this *violet* and *blue,* which thou hast already in part banished and undone. Furthermore, this *orange colour* showeth that the natures are digested, and by little and little perfected by the grace of *God.* As for their Rowl, which saith, *Arise you dead, and come unto the judgment of God my Lord;* I have made it be put there only for the *Theological* sense, rather than any other. It ends in the throat of a *Lion* which is all red, to teach that this operation must not be discontinued until they see the *true red purple,* wholly like unto the *Poppy* of the *Hermitage,* and the *vermillion* of the painted *Lion,* saving for multiplying.

CHAPTER VIII.

The figure of a man, like unto Saint Peter, clothed in a robe Citrine red, holding a key in his right hand, and laying his left hand upon a woman, in an orange-coloured robe, who is on her knees at his feet, holding a Rowl.

LOOK upon this *woman* clothed in a robe of *orange colour,* who doth so naturally resemble *Perrenella* as she was in her youth; She is painted in the fashion of a *suppliant* upon her knees, her hands joined together, at the feet of a *man* who hath a *key* in his *right hand,* who hears her graciously, and afterwards stretcheth out his *left hand* upon her. Wouldst thou know what this meaneth? This is the *Stone,* which in this operation demandeth two things, of the *Mercury of the Sun,* of the *Philosophers,* (painted under the form of a *man*), that is to say, *Multiplication,* and a more rich *Accoutrement:* which at this time it is needful for her to obtain, and therefore the man so laying

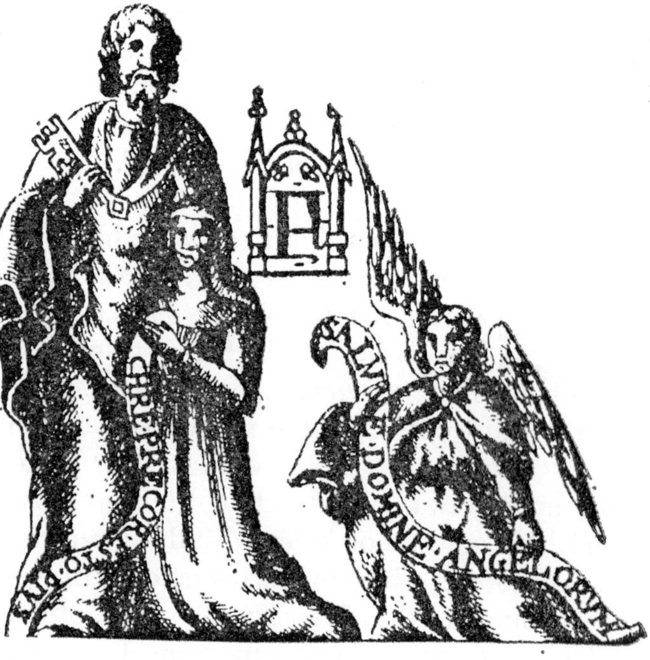
DOMINE ANGELORUM

his hand upon her shoulder accords and grants it unto her. But why have I made to be painted a *woman?* I could as well have made to be painted a *man* as a *woman,* or an *Angel* rather (for the whole natures are now spiritual and corporal, masculine and feminine.) But I have chosen to cause paint a *woman,* to the end that thou mayest judge that she demands rather this than any other thing, because these are the most natural and proper desires of a woman. To show further unto thee that she demandeth *Multiplication,* I have made paint the *man* unto whom she addresseth her prayers in the form of *Saint Peter,* holding a *key,* having power to open and to shut, to bind and to loose; because the envious *Philosophers* have never spoken of *Multiplication* but under these common terms of *Art:—Open, shut, bind, loose; opening* and *loosing;* they have called the making of the *Body* (which is always *hard* and *fixt*), *soft fluid,* and running like water. To *shut* and to *bind* is with them afterwards by a more strong decoction to *coagulate* it, and to bring it back again into the form of a *body.*

F

It behoved me then, in this place to represent a *man* with a *key*, to teach thee that thou must now *open* and *shut*, that is to *Multiply* the budding and increasing natures; for look how often thou shalt dissolve and fix, so often will these natures multiply in *quantity, quality,* and *virtue*, according to the multiplication of *ten:* coming from this number to an *hundred*, from an *hundred* to a *thousand*, from a *thousand* to *ten thousand*, from *ten thousand* to an *hundred thousand*, from an *hundred thousand* to a *million*, and from thence by the same operation to *Infinity*, as I have done three times; praised be *God*. And when thy *Elixir* is so brought unto Infinity one *grain* thereof falling upon a quantity of molten metal as deep and vast as the *Ocean*, it will tein it, and convert it into most perfect *metal;* that is to say, into *silver* or *gold*, according as it shall have been *imbibed* and *fermented*, expelling and driving out far from himself all the impure and strange matter which was joined with the metal in the first *coagulation:* for this reason, therefore, have I made to be painted a *Key* in the hand of the *man*, who is in the form of *Saint Peter*, to signify that the *stone* desireth to be *opened* and *shut* for *multiplication;* and likewise to show thee with what *Mercury* thou oughtest to do this, and when; I have given the man a garment *Citrine red,* and the *woman* one of *orange* colour. Let this suffice —lest I transgress the silence of *Pythagoras*—to teach thee that the *woman,* that is our *stone,* asketh to have the rich Accoutrements and colour of *Saint Peter.* She hath written in her Rowl: *Jesu Christ be pitiful unto me;* as if she said, *Lord be good unto me, and suffer not that he that shall become thus far should spoil all with too much fire. It is true that from henceforward I shall no more fear mine enemies, and that all fire shall be alike unto me, yet the vessel that contains me is always brittle, and easy to be broken: for if they exalt the fire over much it will crack, and, flying apieces, will carry me, and sow me unfortunately amongst the ashes.* Take heed, therefore, to thy fire, in this place, and govern sweetly with patience, this admirable *quintessence;* for the fire must be augmented unto it, but not too much. And pray the sovereign *Goodness* that it will not suffer the evil spirits which keep the *Mines* and *Treasures* to destroy thy work or to bewitch thy *sight*, when thou considerest these incomprehensible motions of this *Quintessence* within thy vessel.

CHAPTER IX.

Upon a dark violet field, a man red purple, holding the feet of a Lion red as vermillion, which hath wings, and it seems would ravish and carry away the man.

THIS field, *violet* and *dark*, tells us that the *stone* hath obtained by her full decoction the fair *garments* that are wholly *Citrine* and *red* which she demanded of *Saint Peter*, who was clothed therewith, and that her complete and perfect *digestion* (signified by the entire *Citrinity*) hath made her leave her old robe of *orange colour*. The *vermillion* red colour of this *flying Lion*, like the pure and clear *Scarlet* in grain, which is of the tone *Granadored*, demonstrates that it is now accomplished in all right and equality. And that she is now like a *Lion*, devouring every pure and *metallic* nature, and changing it into her true substance, into true and pure *Gold*, more fine than that of the best mines. Also, she now carrieth this man out of this vale of miseries, that is to say, out of the discommodities of *poverty* and *infirmity*, and with her wings gloriously lifts him up, out of the dead and standing waters of *Egypt* (which are the ordinary thoughts of mortal men) making him despise this life, and the riches thereof, causing him night and day to meditate on *God*, and his *Saints*, to dwell in the *Imperial Heaven*, and to drink the sweet springs of the Fountains of *everlasting hope*. Praised be *God* eternally, who hath given us grace to see this most pure and all perfect *purple* colour; this pleasant colour of the *wild poppy* of the *Rock*, this *Tyrian* sparkling and flaming colour, which is incapable of *Alteration* or *change*, over which the *heaven* itself nor his *Zodiac* can have no domination nor power, whose bright shining rays, that dazzle the eyes, seem as though they did communicate unto a man some super-celestial things, making him (when he beholds and knows it) to be astonished, to tremble, and to be afraid at the same time.

O Lord, give us grace to use it well, to the augmentation of the Faith, and the profit of our Souls, and to the increase of the glory of this noble Realm.

AMEN

THE TEXT OF THE *Alchemical Hieroglyphics* OF NICHOLAS FLAMMEL HAS BEEN SET BY LINOTYPE IN FOURTEEN POINT GARAMOUND BY TYPOGRAPHIC ASSOCIATES OF ISELIN NEW JERSEY ❧PLATES FOR THE ILLUSTRATIONS WERE PHOTO-ENGRAVED BY VAN-ALLYN GRAPHICS OF NEW YORK CITY ❧PRINTED LETTERPRESS & BOUND BY HEPTANGLE BOOKS IN THE PASSAIC VALLEY AT GILLETTE NEW JERSEY